Humility: The Least of All the Saints
By Thomas Brooks
Edited by Dustin Benge

© 2021 by Dustin Benge

Published by: H&E Publishing, Peterbourough, Ontario
www.hesedandemet.com

All rights reserved. This book or any portion thereof may not be reproduced or used in any manner whatsoever without the express written permission of the publisher except for the use of brief quotations in a book review.

Source in Public Domain: Thomas Brooks, *The Complete Works of Thomas Brooks*, vol. 3 (Edinburgh: James Nichol, 1866).

Thomas Brooks, *The Complete Works of Thomas Brooks*, vol. 1 (Edinburgh: James Nichol, 1866).

See also: Thomas Brooks, *The Complete Works of Thomas Brooks*, vol. 3 (Edinburgh, The Banner of Truth Trust, 1980.

Scripture quotations are from The ESV® Bible (The Holy Bible, English Standard Version®), copyright © 2001 by Crossway, a publishing ministry of Good News Publishers. Used by permission. All rights reserved.

Cover painting: *Wooded Hillside with a Vista*, 1645 by Jan Both

Design and layout: Dustin Benge

Paperback ISBN: 978-1-77484-001-6
EBook ISBN: 978-1-77484-002-3

First edition, 2021

HUMILITY

The Least of All the Saints

THOMAS BROOKS

Edited by Dustin Benge

CONTENTS

	Biography: The Life and Ministry of Thomas Brooks	7
	Preface	13
1	The Most Holy Are Always the Most Humble	17
2	The Reasons Why the Best Are the Most Humble	53
3	The Motives of Humility	61
4	Help and Direction in the Way of Humility	75
5	Concerning Pride	87
6	Be Clothed With Humility	103

"He leads the humble in what is right, and teaches the humble his way."

PSALM 25:9

BIOGRAPHY

The Life and Ministry of Thomas Brooks

Much of what we know about Thomas Brooks (1608–1680) is discovered from his writings. Born in 1608, nothing is known of his childhood or early influences. Brooks entered Emmanuel College in Cambridge on July 7, 1625, where he was preceded by such men as Thomas Hooker (1586–1647), John Cotton (1585–1652), and Thomas Shephard (1605–1649), all three of which eventually sailed to the colonies of the new world. Brooks never flaunts his degrees from Cambridge choosing rather instead to be known as a "preacher of the gospel" and "preacher of the Word."

Brooks was licensed to preach the gospel in 1640. By 1648, he had become minister at Thomas Apostle's in London just after the ending of the First English Civil War in

1646. He delivered a sermon before the House of Commons on December 26, 1648, which brought him sufficient renown. His sermon title was, "God's Delight in the Progress of the Upright," choosing his text from Psalm 44:18, "Our heart has not turned back, nor have our steps departed from your way." After three to four years at Thomas Apostle's, he transferred to St. Margaret's, Fish-street Hill, London. Charles Spurgeon said of him, "Brooks scatters stars with both hands, with an eagle eye of faith as well as the eagle eye of imagination" (Preface to *Smooth Stones, taken from Ancient Brooks*, by Thomas Brooks).

In 1662, he, along with numerous other Puritan preachers and pastors, fell victim to the Act of Uniformity, but it appears he was able to retain his pulpit and preached when opportunities arose. Regardless, treatises continued to flow from his pen. From the six volumes of his complete works, some of his most remembered treaties include, *Precious Remedies Against Satan's Devices*, *The Secret Key to Heaven*, *Heaven on Earth: A Treatise on Christian Assurance*, and *Smooth Stones Taken from Ancient Brooks*.

What follows are the "personal endowments" or characteristics of Thomas Brooks as a man and minister of the gospel of Christ. Chronicled by Alexander B. Grosart who sketched together the following memoir of Brooks in the first volume of his collected works, these characteristics help to construct a portrait of a man who we know very little about biographically.

1. *A person of a very sweet nature and temper.* So affable, and courteous, and cheerful, that he gained upon all that conversed with him. And if any taxed him with any pride or moroseness, it must be only such as did not know him. He had so winning a way with him that he might bid himself welcome into whatsoever house he entered. Pride and moroseness are bad qualities for a man of his employ, and make men afraid of the ways of God, for fear they should never enjoy a good day after.

2. *A person of a very great gravity.* He could carry a majesty in his face when there was occasion and make the least guilt tremble in his presence with his very countenance. I never knew a man better loved, nor more dreaded. God had given him such a spirit with power, that his very frowns were darts, and his reproofs sharper than swords. He would not contemn familiarity but hated that familiarity that bred contempt.

3. *A person of a very large charity.* He had a large heart and a great dexterity in the opening of the hearts of others, as well as his own to works of mercy that I think I may say there is not a Church in England that hath more often and more liberal contributions for poor ministers and other poor Christians than this is, according to the proportion of their abilities.

4. *A person of wonderful patience.* Notwithstanding the many weaknesses and infirmities, which for a long time have been continually, without ceasing as it were, trying

their skill to pull down his frail body to the dust, and at last effected it, yet I never heard an impatient word drop from him. When I came to visit him, and asked him, "How do you, Sir?" He answered, "Pretty well. I bless God I am well, I am contented with the will of my Father. My Father's will and mine are but one will." It made me often think that Isaiah 33:24, "No inhabitant will say, 'I am sick;' the people who dwell there will be forgiven their iniquity." Sense of pardon took away sense of sickness.

5. *A person of a very strong faith in the promises of both worlds.* He could not be otherwise being a continual student of the covenant. He feared nothing of himself or others, knowing the promise and oath of God would stand firm, and the Head of the Church would see to the safety of all his members, here and hereafter.

For his ministerial endowments, he was:

1. *An experienced minister.* From the heart to the heart. From the conscience to the conscience. He had a body of divinity in his head, and the power of it upon his heart.

2. *A laborious minister.* As his works in press and pulpit are undeniable witness of. To preach so often, and print so much, and yet not satisfied till he could imprint also his works upon the hearts of his people, which is the best way of printing that I know, and the greatest task of a minister of Christ.

3. *He was a minister who delighted in his work.* It was his meat and drink to labor in that great work, insomuch that

under his weakness he would be often preaching of little sermons—as he called them—to those that came to visit him, even when by reason of his distemper that were very hardly able to understand them.

4. *He was a successful minister.* He was the instrument in the hand of God for the conversion of many souls about this city (London) and elsewhere.

5. *And now he is at rest.* And though he is gone, he is not lost. He is yet useful to the church of God and being dead he yet speaks by his example and writings, which were very profitable and spiritual.

This modest, unexaggerated, heart-full portraiture is worthy of the man as the man was, with emphasis, worthy of it.[1]

---

[1] Alexander B. Grosart, "Memoir of Thomas Brooks," in *The Complete Works of Thomas Brooks*, vol. 1 (Edinburgh: The Banner of Truth Trust, 1980), 36–37.

"For everyone who exalts himself will be humbled, and he who humbles himself will be exalted."

LUKE 14:11

PREFACE

Dustin Benge

We live in a culture where humility isn't viewed as a noble virtue but debasing characteristic reserved for the weak, naïve, and venerable. We've become accustomed to the injunction that if "you aren't first, push your way through the crowd until you are." However, this is not the message of Scripture.

In Isaiah 66, the Lord tells us that he is looking for humble people, "…the one to whom I will look: he who is humble and contrite in spirit and trembles at my word" (Isa. 66:2). God is looking for humble people. The prophet Micah instructs us that the Lord desires those who "walk humbly" with him (Mic. 6:8). Jesus echoes these words when he teaches the parable of the wedding feast. He says, "For everyone who exalts himself will be humbled, and he who humbles himself will be exalted" (Luke 14:11). And Paul commands believers to "put on…humility" (Col. 3:12). In a culture filled with pride and self-aggrandizement, believers need to remember the words of Scripture to walk in humility.

Throughout the life of Christ, we see example after example of what it looks like to walk in true humility—birth in a manger, having no place to lay his head, washing feet, touching lepers. The greatest act of humility in the history of the world was the example Christ sets forth in his emptying of himself and subjecting himself to the painful agony of sin-bearing upon the cross. Paul noted in Philippians 2:8 that "being found in human form, he humbled himself by becoming obedient to the point of death, even death on a cross." Therefore, Christ is the ultimate act of humility and is consequently the preeminent example to all who desire to "put on" the same humility.

Thomas Brooks said, "Oh! Labor every day to be more humble and more low and little in your own eyes." A significant concern for Brooks was how believers viewed themselves after they became Christians. After all, inheriting eternal life, gaining the riches of grace, being in favor with God may cause the recipient to be puffed up with pride, much like the Pharisees and religious leaders of the New Testament. But for Brooks, the true Christian is more willing to wash the feet of others than to have his feet washed. The believer who desires to walk in humility views themselves through the lens of Christ, who bore the cross in shame and disgrace to purchase salvation for sinners. A humble heart serves. A humble heart loves. A humble heart recognizes that not even a crumb of mercy is deserved.

You are about to embark on a journey of the soul. Brooks enters every room of your heart and applies Scripture to clean out the cobwebs of bitterness, pride, and self-righteousness. Before beginning this journey, ask God to reveal areas of your life where you lack humility and refuse to manifest the characteristics of humility toward others. You will be challenged, changed, and connected to the fountain from which all humility flows.

"The reward for humility

and fear of the Lord is

riches and honor

and life."

PROVERBS 22:4

ONE

The Most Holy Are Always the Most Humble

I shall begin with the first words, "To me, though I am the very least of all the saints." Two observations naturally flow from these words. First, that the holiest men are always the most humble men. None are so humble on earth as those who live highest in heaven. It could also be said this way: That those who are the most highly valued and esteemed of by God are lowest and least in their own estimation and that there are weak saints as well as strong, little saints as well as great. Or to say it another way: All saints are not of equal growth or stature.

I shall begin with the first observation that the holiest men are always the most humble men. Souls that are the most highly esteemed and valued by God set the least and

HUMILITY

lowest esteem upon themselves. Paul said, "To me, though I am the very least of all the saints" (Eph. 3:8).

Job was humble in regard to those perfections and degrees of grace which he had attained to beyond any other saints on earth. No man ever received a fairer or a more valuable certificate under the hand of God, or the broad seal of heaven, for his being a soul famous in grace and holiness than Job. "And the Lord said to Satan, 'Have you considered my servant Job, that there is none like him on the earth, a blameless and upright man, who fears God and turns away from evil?'" (Job 1:8). No man could speak more lowly of himself than Job did. "I had heard of you by the hearing of the ear, but now my eye sees you; therefore I despise myself, and repent in dust and ashes" (Job 42:5–6). Job was high in worth and humble in heart. This expression is the deepest act of abhorrence. Abhorrence strictly taken is hatred wound up to the height. "I despise myself." The word that is rendered "despise" signifies to reject, to disdain, and to cast off. "Ah!" says Job, "I despise myself, I reject myself, I disdain myself, I cast off myself, I have a vile esteem of myself.

The apostle Paul, who had been caught up into the third heavens and had such glorious revelations as could not be uttered yet, accounted himself less than the least of all the saints. Not that anything can be less than the least, but Paul means he was as little as could be. Therefore, he put himself down so little as could not be, less than the least.

Another proof is found in the prophet Isaiah. As Paul, among the apostles, was the greatest, so Isaiah, among the prophets, was the clearest and choicest gospel preacher and holds out more of Christ and of his kingdom and glory than all the other prophets do. In Isaiah 6:1, Isaiah sees the glory of the Lord in a vision, and this makes him cry out in verse 5, "Woe is me! For I am lost; for I am a man of unclean lips, and I dwell in the midst of a people of unclean lips; for my eyes have seen the King, the Lord of hosts!" "For I am lost and cut off, I am a forlorn man!" Why? "For my eyes have seen the King, the Lord of hosts!" The clearest sight and vision of God does always give a man the fullest sight of his own emptiness, sinfulness, and nothingness. Here you have the highest and choicest among the prophets, as you had Paul before among the apostles, abasing and laying low himself.

Another example is the apostle Peter who says, "Depart from me, for I am a sinful man, O Lord" (Luke 5:8). That is a man, a sinner—a compound of dirt and sin. When he saw that glorious miracle wrought by the Lord Jesus, he cries out as one very sensible of his own weakness and sinfulness, "Depart from me, for I am a sinful man." He was saying, "I am not worthy to be near such majesty and glory, who am a mere bundle of vice and vanity, of folly and iniquity!"

Take another clear instance in Genesis 18:27, "Abraham answered and said, "Behold, I have undertaken to speak to the Lord, I who am but dust and ashes." Here you have the father of the faithful, the greatest believer in the world, accounting himself dust and ashes. Dust notes the baseness of his original and ashes notes his deserving to be burnt to ashes—if God should deal with him in justice rather than in mercy. The nearer any soul draws to God; the more humble will that soul lie before God. None so near God as the angels, nor any so humble before God as the angels.

The same can be said of Jacob: "I am not worthy of the least of all the deeds of steadfast love and all the faithfulness that you have shown to your servant" (Gen. 32:10). Jacob, a man eminent in his prevailing with God, a prince that had the honor and the happiness to overcome the God of mercy—yet judges himself unworthy of the least mercy. How low is that soul in his own eyes who is most honorable in God's eyes!

You know David was a man after God's own heart (1 Kings 15:5). A man highly honored, much beloved, and dearly prized by the Lord. Yet in 1 Samuel 26:20, he counts himself a flea; and what is more contemptible than a flea? In Psalm 22:6, he says, "I am a worm and not a man." The word that is there rendered worm is a word that signifies a very little worm—a worm that is so little that a man can hardly see or perceive it. A worm is the most despicable creature in the world, trampled underfoot by everyone. David says, "I am a despicable worm in my own eyes. A humble soul is a little, little nothing in his own eyes."

Thus, you see the point proved that the holiest men have always been the most humble men.

The second thing that I am to do is to show you the properties of humble souls. I confess, when I look abroad in the world and observe the demeanor of all sorts of men, my heart is stirred to speak as fully and as home to this point, as Christ shall help me. It is very sad to consider how few humble souls there are in these days—the damnable pride that reigns and rules in the hearts and lives of most men. I think it is far greater than has been known in the generations before us.

1. A Humble Soul Never Forgets His Sinfulness

Paul had been taken up into the third heavens and had glorious revelations and manifestations of God (2 Cor. 12:1–4). He cries out, "I was a blasphemer, persecutor, and insolent opponent" (1 Tim. 1:13). Under the choicest discoveries, he remembers his former blasphemies: "I see in my members another law waging war against the law of my mind and making me captive to the law of sin that dwells in my members" (Rom. 7:23). He had been at this time about fourteen years converted. He was a man who lived at as high a rate in God as any we read of. A man who was filled with glorious spiritual discoveries and revelations and yet under all discoveries and revelations, he remembers that body of sin and death that made him cry out, "O wretched man that I am, who shall deliver me?" Who shall ease me of my burden? Who shall knock off these chains that make my life a hell? Although Paul had obtained pardon of God for his sins, yet he is not ashamed to admit his personal wretchedness to the world.

I will by a few instances prove the other branch: "I am not worthy of the least of all the deeds of steadfast love," says Jacob, "for with my staff I crossed this Jordan, and now I have become two camps" (Gen. 32:10). He said, "I went over Jordan and was as a footman that carried all his wealth with him." Under his outward greatness, he forgets not his former baseness. A humble soul is good at looking back upon his former low estate, upon his threadbare coat, which was his best and only robe.

Also David: "Then King David went in and sat before the Lord and said, "Who am I, O Lord God, and what is my house, that you have brought me thus far? And this was a small thing in your eyes, O God. You have also spoken of your servant's house for a great while to come, and have shown me future generations, O Lord God!" (1 Chron. 17:16–17). David remembered the baseness of his birth. He remembered his shepherd's crook, as Jacob did his traveling staff.

God's mercies make a humble soul glad, but not proud. A humble soul is lowest when his mercies are highest. He is least when he is greatest. He is lowest when he is highest. He is most poor when he is most rich. Nothing melts like mercy. Nothing draws like mercy. Nothing humbles like mercy. Mercy gives the humble soul such excellent counsel. The voice of mercy is, "Remember what you once were, and what now you are, and be humble."

Now proud men who are lifted up from the ash-heap, who abound in worldly wealth, how does their blood rise with their outward good! The more mercies they have, the prouder they are. Mercies do but puff and swell such souls. In a crowd of mercies, they cry out in the pride of their hearts: "They say to God, 'Depart from us! We do not desire the knowledge of your ways. What is the Almighty, that we should serve him? And what profit do we get if we pray to him?'" (Job 21:14–15).

2. A Humble Soul Lives Upon the Righteousness of Christ

The apostle Paul, in Philippians 3:8–10, overlooks his own righteousness and lives wholly upon the righteousness of Christ: "I desire to be found in him," he says, "not having my own righteousness." Away with it! It is dross. It is dung. It is dog meat! It is rotten righteousness, imperfect righteousness, weak righteousness, which is of the law. But that which is through the faith of Christ, the righteousness which is from God by faith—that is spotless righteousness, pure righteousness, complete righteousness, incomparable righteousness! Therefore, a humble soul overlooks his own righteousness and lives upon Christ's righteousness.

Remember this: all the sighing, mourning, sobbing, and

complaining in the world does not so undeniably evidence a man to be humble, as his overlooking his own righteousness, and living really and purely upon the righteousness of Christ. Men may do much, hear much, pray much, fast much, and give much, and yet be as proud as Lucifer, as you may see in the Scribes and Pharisees in Matthew 23, and those in Isaiah 58:3, who in the pride of their hearts made an idol of their own righteousness: "Why have we fasted," they say, "and you see it not? Why have we humbled ourselves, and you take no knowledge of it?" Oh! For a man now to trample upon his own righteousness and to live wholly upon the righteousness of another, this speaks out a man to be humble indeed. There is nothing that the heart of man stands more averse to than this—discarding his own righteousness. Man is a creature apt to warm himself with the sparks of his own fire, though he does lie down for it in eternal sorrow (Isa. 50:11). Man is naturally prone to go about to establish his own righteousness, that he might not subject to the righteousness of Christ. He will labor as for life, to lift up his own righteousness, and to make a Savior of it (Rom. 10:4).

But a humble soul disclaims his own righteousness: "All our righteousness is as filthy rags." "Enter not into judgment with your servant, for no one living is righteous before you" (Ps. 143:2). Job said, "Though I am in the right, I cannot answer him; I must appeal for mercy to my accuser" (Job 9:15). Proud Pharisees bless themselves in their own righteousness: "I thank you that I am not like other men...I fast twice a week..." (Luke 18:11–12). But now, a soul truly humbled blushes to see his own righteousness and glories in this, that he has the righteousness of Christ to live upon. A proud heart eyes more his seeming worth than his real needs. In Revelation 4:10–11, the twenty-four elders throw down their crowns at the feet of Christ. By their crowns, you may understand their gifts, their excellencies, their righteousness. They throw down these before Christ's throne to note to us that they did not put confidence in them and that Christ was the crown of crowns and the top of all their royalty and glory. A humble soul looks upon Christ's righteousness as his only crown.

3. A Humble Soul Performs Good Works

A humble David will dance before the ark. He enjoyed so much of God in it that it caused him to leap and dance before it. But Michal, his wife, despised him for a fool and counted him as a simple vain fellow, looking upon his behavior as vain and light and not becoming the might, majesty, and glory of so glorious a prince. "Well," says this humble soul, "if this be to be vile, I will be more vile!"

Paul, yet being humble and low in his own eyes, can stoop to do service to the least and lowest saint.

For though I am free from all, I have made myself a servant to all, that I might win more of them. To the Jews, I became a Jew in order to win Jews. To those under the law,

I became as one under the law (though not being myself under the law) that I might win those under the law. To those outside the law, I became as one outside the law (not being outside the law of God but under the law of Christ) that I might win those outside the law. To the weak, I became weak, that I might win the weak. I have become all things to all people, that by all means, I might save some (1 Cor. 9:19–22).

"Ah," says Paul, "it is my greatest joy, my greatest delight, to gain souls to Christ." The word win signifies craft or guile. Humble Paul will use a holy craft, holy guile, to win souls. Here you have a humble soul bowing and stooping to the lowest saint and the lowest services that he might win souls.

So, the Lord Jesus himself was famous in this (John 13:4). Though he was the Lord of glory, and one who thought it no robbery to be equal with God, one who had all perfection and fullness in himself, yet the lowest work is not below this King of kings. Witness his washing his disciples' feet and wiping them with a towel (1 Cor. 2:8; Phil. 2:6; Col. 1:19).

Bonaventure, though he was born of great pedigree and a great scholar, yet to keep his mind from swelling, would often sweep rooms, wash dishes, and make beds. So that famous Italian marquees, when God was pleased by the ministry of his word to convert him, the lowest work was not below him. Though he might have lived like a king in his own country, yet having tasted of that life and sweetness which are in Jesus, he was so humble that he would go to the market and carry home the cheapest and the poorest things the market yielded. There was nothing below him when God had changed and humbled him. Proud hearts cannot stoop to low services. They say this work and that is below their abilities, station, parentage, and employments.

It was recorded to the glory of some ancient generals that they were able to call every common soldier by his own name and were careful to provide money, not only for their captains and soldiers but litter also for the basest animal. These heathens will rise in judgment against many proud professors these days who scorn to stoop to low services. So, it is with all that is high in worth and humble in heart. God will be sanctified either actively or passively, either in us or upon us (Lev. 10:2–3). There is not the lowest good work, which is below the humble soul. If the work is good, though ever so low, humility will put a hand to it, but pride will not so much as touch it.

4. A Humble Soul Submits to God's Truth

In 1 Samuel 3:17, Eli would sincerely know what God had revealed to Samuel concerning him. Samuel tells him that he must break his neck, that the priesthood must be taken away from him, and his sons must be slain in the war. "It is the Lord," he says, "let him do what seems him good."

HUMILITY

In Leviticus 10:3, the Lord destroys Aaron's two sons by fire from heaven, "Aaron held his peace." If God misses of his honor one way, he will rain hell out of heaven—but he will have it another way. Aaron knew this, and therefore he remained silent when God showed himself to be "a consuming fire." The Hebrew word that is here rendered "silent" signifies the quietness and silence of his mind. The word often signifies a modest quietness of mind, the troubled affections being dispelled. In Lamentations 3:27–29, it signifies to submit unto God and to be patient in affliction, and so it may be taken here.

He did not hold his tongue only, for many a man may hold his tongue, and yet his mind and heart may kick and swell against God, but his very mind was quiet and still. There was a heavenly calm in his spirit. He was quiet and silent because the Lord had done it. In Acts 10:33, "We are all here in the presence of God to hear all that you have been commanded by the Lord." We are not here to hear what may tickle our ears, or please our fancies, or satisfy our lusts. No, but we are here to hear what God will say. Our hearts stand ready pressed to subject themselves to whatever God shall declare to be his will. We are willing to hear what we may do, that we may obey sincerely and universally the good pleasure of our God, knowing that it is as well our dignity as our duty so to do.

There are three things in a humble soul, which do strongly incline it to duty. The first is divine love. The second is the divine presence. The third is divine glory.

The dove made use of her wings to fly to the ark; so does a humble soul of his duties to fly to Christ. Though the dove did use her wings, yet she did not trust in her wings but in the ark. So though a humble soul does use duties, yet he does not trust in his duties, but in his Jesus. But now proud hearts they hate the truth, they cry out, "Who is the Lord, that we should obey him?" And what are his commandments that we should submit to them? A truly humble soul falls under the power of truth and counts it his greatest glory to be obedient to all truth.

5. A Humble Soul Lives Upon Christ

Poor men do not live upon themselves; they live upon others. They live upon the care of others, the love of others, and the provision of others. Why thus a humble soul lives upon the care of Christ, the love of Christ, the promise of Christ, the faithfulness of Christ, and the discoveries of Christ. He lives upon Christ for his justification (Phil. 3:7–10).

He lives upon Christ for his sanctification, "Awake, O north wind, and come, O south wind! Blow upon my garden, let its spices flow" (Song of Sol. 4:16). And he also lives upon Christ for his consolation, "As an apple tree among the trees of the forest, so is my beloved among the young men. With great delight I sat in his shadow, and his fruit was sweet to my taste" (Song of Sol. 2:3). And he lives upon Christ for the performance of all holy actions, "I can do all things through Christ who strengthens me" (Phil 4:13); "I have been crucified with Christ. It is no longer I who live, but Christ who lives in me" (Gal. 2:20).

A humble soul sees in Christ a fullness of abundance and fullness of redundancy, and here his soul lives and feeds. A humble soul sees that all his stock of blessings is in the hands of Christ. His stock of graces, his stock of comforts, his stock of experiences are in the hands of Jesus Christ, who is the great Lord and keeper of all a believer's graces and of all his comforts.

Therefore, as children live upon the hand of their parents, so a humble soul sees its stock of blessings are in the hand of the Lord Jesus, and therefore he lives upon Christ—upon his love, and his provision, and his undertakings.

Proud hearts live not upon the Lord Jesus Christ. They live upon themselves, and upon their own duties, their own righteousness, their own actings, as the Scripture evidence. Christ dwells in that heart most eminently, that has emptied itself of itself. Christ is the humble man's manna upon which he lives and by which he thrives (Isa. 58:2, 7; Luke 7:47).

6. A Humble Soul Recognizes He Deserves Judgment

A proud heart resists and is resisted: flint to flint, fire to fire. A humble soul blesses God as well for crosses as mercies, as well for adversity as for prosperity, as well for frowns as for smiles, because he judges himself unworthy of the least rebukes from God. A humble soul looks upon himself as one not worthy that God should spend a rod upon him in order to his reformation, edification, or salvation. "As I am unworthy," a humble soul says, "that God should smile upon me, so I am unworthy that he should spend a frown upon me." "Will you frighten a driven leaf and pursue dry chaff?" (Job 13:25). Why I am but a leaf, I am but a little dry stubble, I am below your wrath; I am so very, very bad, that I wonder that you should so much as spend a rod upon me. What more weak, worthless, slight, and contemptible than a leaf, than dry stubble? "Why, Lord," Job says, "I am a poor, weak, and worthless creature, I wonder that you should take any pains to do me good, I can't but count and call everything a mercy—which is less than I deserve—which is less than hell."

David, in 1 Samuel 24:14, "After whom has the king of Israel come out? After whom do you pursue? After a dead dog! After a flea!" The language of a humble soul, when God begins to be angry, is this: "Lord, I can bless you who you will take any pains with me; but I humbly acknowledge that I am below the least rod, I am not worthy that you should frown upon me, threaten me, strike me, or whip me, for my internal and eternal good."

Proud hearts think themselves wronged when they are afflicted. They cry out with Cain, "My punishment is greater than I can bear" (Gen. 4:13).

7. A Humble Soul Prizes Christ

The Canaanite woman in the fifteenth chapter of Matthew sets a high price upon a crumb of mercy. Faith will pick an argument out of a repulse and turn discouragements into encouragements. Martin Luther would not take all the world for one leaf of the Bible; such a price he set upon it, from the sweet that he found in it. "Ah, Lord," the humble soul says, "if I may not have a loaf of mercy, give me a piece of mercy; if not a piece of mercy, give me a crumb of mercy. If I may not have sun-light, let me have moon-light; if not moon-light, let me have star-light; if not star-light, let me have candle-light; and for that, I will bless you."

In the time of the law, the lowest things that were consecrated for use in the tabernacle were very highly prized—such as leather or wood. A humble soul looks upon all the things of God as consecrated things. Every truth of God is a consecrated truth; it is consecrated to a holy use, and this causes the soul highly to prize it. And so, every smile of God, and every discovery of God, and every drop of mercy from God is very highly prized by a soul that walks humbly with God. The name of Christ, the voice of Christ, the footsteps of Christ, the least touch of the garment of Christ, the least-regarded truth of Christ, the lowest and least-regarded among the flock of Christ, is highly prized by humble souls that are savingly interested in Christ (Song of Sol. 1:3; John 10:4–5; Ps. 27:4; Matt. 9:20–21; Acts 24:14; 1 Cor. 9:22).

A humble soul cannot, a humble soul dares not, call anything little which has Christ in it. Neither can a humble soul call nor count anything great wherein he sees not Christ, wherein he enjoys not Christ. A humble soul highly prizes the least nod, the least love-token, and the least courtesy from Christ. But proud hearts count great mercies small mercies, and small mercies no mercies; yes, pride does so unman them, that they often call mercy misery.

8. A Humble Soul Strives for Godliness

Humble Paul looks upon his greatness as nothing at all. He forgets those things which are behind and reaches forth to those things which are before, "that by any means possible I may attain the resurrection from the dead" (Phil. 3:11-14). That is that perfection of holiness which the dead shall attain unto in the morning of the resurrection. It signifies the straining of the whole body, a stretching out head and hands, as runners in a race do to lay hold on the prize (Ps. 10:17). It signifies so to desire and long after a thing as to have one's teeth water at it (Mic. 7:1).

Proud hearts sit down and pride themselves and bless themselves as if they had attained too much when they have attained to nothing which can raise them above the lowest step of misery.

HUMILITY

No holiness below that matchless, peerless, spotless, perfect holiness that saints shall have in the glorious day of Christ's appearing will satisfy the humble soul. A humble heart is an aspiring heart. He cannot be contented to get up some rounds in Jacob's ladder. He must get to the very top of the ladder, to the very top of holiness. A humble heart cannot be satisfied with so much grace as will bring him to glory, with so much of heaven as will keep him from dropping into hell. He is still crying out, "Give, Lord, give; give me more of yourself, more of your Son, more of your Spirit; give me more light, more life, more love." Caesar, in warlike matters, minded more what was to conquer than what was already conquered; what was to gain than what was already gained. So makes a humble soul mind more what he should be than what he is; what is to be done than what has been done. Truly heaven is for that man, and that man is for heaven, that sets up for his mark the perfection of holiness.

Poor men are full of desires. They are often crying out, "Oh, that we had bread to strengthen us, drink to refresh us, clothes to cover us, friends to visit us, and houses to shelter us. So souls that are spiritually poor are often a-sighing it out, Oh that we had more of Christ to strengthen us, more of Christ to refresh us, more of Christ to be a covering and shelter to us. "I had rather," says the humble soul, "be a poor man and a rich Christian than a rich man and a poor Christian." "Lord," says the humble soul, "I had rather do anything, I had rather bear anything, I had rather be anything, than to be a dwarf in grace" (Rev. 3:17; Isa. 65:5; Luke 18:11–12).

The light and glory of humble Christians rise by degrees: 1. Looking forth as the morning, with a little light; 2. Fair as the moon, more light; 3. Clear as the sun that is come up to a higher degree of spiritual light, life, and glory (Song of Sol. 6:1).

9. A Humble Soul Mortifies Sin

When David had but cut off the hem of Saul's garment, his heart smote him as if he had cut off his head. The Hebrew word signifies smite, wound, or chastise. A good man's heart, when kindly awakened, may smite him for those actions which at first he judged very prudent and correct (1 Sam. 24:5). How great a pain, not to be borne, comes from the prick of this small thorn! Little sins have put several to their wits' ends when they have been set home upon their consciences. His heart struck him. His heart chastised him. His heart wounded him for cutting off Saul's skirt, though he did it upon noble grounds, namely, to convince Saul of his false jealousies and to evidence his own innocence and integrity. And so, at another time, his heart smote him for numbering the people—as if he had murdered the people: "Behold, this day your eyes have seen how the Lord gave you today into my hand in the cave. And some told me to kill you, but I spared you. I said, 'I will not put out my hand against my lord, for he is the Lord's anointed'" (2 Sam. 24:10).

A humble soul knows that little sins, if I may so call any, cost Christ his blood; and that they make way for greater sins; and that little sins multiplied become great, as a little sum multiplied is great. He knows that little sins cloud the face of God, wound conscience, grieve the Spirit, rejoice Satan, and do work for repentance. A humble soul knows that little sins are very dangerous. A little leaven leavens the whole lump. A little blow may kill one. A little poison may poison another. A little leak in a ship sinks it. A little fly in the box of ointment spoils it. A little flaw in a good project mars it. So a little sin may at once bar the door of heaven and open the gates of hell. Therefore, a humble soul smites and upbraids itself for the least as well as the greatest sins. Though ahead of garlic be little, yet it will poison the leopard, though he is great. Though a mouse is but little, yet it will kill an elephant if he gets up into his trunk. Though the scorpion is little, yet it will sting a lion to death, and so will the least sin, if not pardoned by the death of Christ.

A proud heart counts great sins small, and small sins no sins, and so disarms conscience for a time of its whipping and wounding power; but at death, or in hell, conscience will take up an iron rod, with which it will lash the sinner forever. Then, though too late, the sinner shall acknowledge his little sins to be very great and his great sins to be exceeding grievous and odious.

10. A Humble Soul Bears Burdens

A humble soul sees God through man. He sees God through all the actions and behaviors of men. A humble soul looks through secondary causes and sees the hand of God, and then lays his own hand upon his mouth. A humble soul is a mute soul, a tongue-tied soul when he looks through secondary causes to the supreme cause. Aaron, when he saw his sons suddenly surprised by a dreadful and doleful death, he remained silent. He bridled his passions. He sits silently under a terrible stroke of divine justice because the fire that devoured them went out from the Lord. So when Samuel had told Eli that God would judge his house forever and that he had sworn that the iniquity of his house should not be purged with sacrifice nor offering forever, "It is the Lord," says Eli, "let him do what seems good unto him." Eli humbly and patiently lays his neck upon the block, "it is the Lord; let him strike, let him kill," Eli says (1 Sam. 3:11, 13).

So David, when Shimei manifested his desperate fury and folly, malice and madness, in raving and raging at him, in cursing and reproaching of him, he says, "Let him alone, and let him curse, for the Lord has bidden him," (2 Sam. 16:5, 10). "God," David says, "will, by his wise providence, turn his cursing into blessing. I see the justice of God in his cursing, therefore let him alone, let him curse."

HUMILITY

So that blessed martyr, Gyles of Brussels, whenever the friars abused him, he ever remained silent, insomuch that those wretches would say abroad that he had a dumb devil in him. Full vessels will bear many a knock, many a stroke, and yet make no noise. So Christians who are full of Christ, who are full of the Spirit, will bear many a knock, many a stroke, and yet make no noise.

A humble soul may groan under afflictions, but he will not grumble in calms. Proud hearts discourse about patience, but in storms, humble hearts exercise patience. Philosophers have much commended patience, but in the hour of darkness, it is the humble soul who acts patient. "I am afflicted," the humble soul says, "but it is mercy I am not destroyed. I am fallen into the pit—but it is free grace that I have not fallen into hell. God is too just to wrong me and too gracious to harm me, and therefore I will be still and quiet, let him do what he will with me."

Proud souls resist when they are resisted, they strike when they are stricken (Isa. 58:1–3). "Who is the Lord," says lofty Pharaoh, "that I should obey him?" (Ex. 5:2). Cain cries out, "My punishment is greater than I am able to bear" (Gen. 4:13).

Well, remember this: though it is not easy in afflictions and tribulations to remain quiet and silent, yet it is very advantageous. Those who do prudently and humbly conceal their sorrows and anxieties by patience shall attain comfort and refreshment.

11. A Humble Soul Depends Fully Upon Christ

"Lord," the humble soul says, "I need power against such and such sins. Give it to me upon the credit of Christ's blood. I need strength to such and such services. Give it to me upon the credit of Christ's word. I need such and such mercies for my cheering, refreshing, quickening, and strengthening. Give them into my bosom upon the credit of Christ's intercession." As a poor man lives and deals upon the credits of others, so does a humble soul live and deal with God for the strengthening of every grace and for the supply of every mercy upon the credit of the Lord Jesus. A humble soul knows that since he broke with God in innocency, God will trust him no more. He will take his word no more. Therefore, when he goes to God for mercy, he brings Jesus in his arms and pleads for mercy upon the account of Jesus.

Humble souls make a conquest upon God with Christ in their arms. The Father will not give that soul the repulse, who brings Christ in his arms. The humble soul knows that outside of Christ, God is incommunicable. Outside of Christ, God is incomprehensible. Outside of Christ, God is very dreadful. Outside of Christ, God is inaccessible. Therefore, he still brings Christ with him, and presents all his requests in his name, and so prevails. Oh, but proud souls deal with God upon the credit of their own worthiness, righteousness, services, prayers, tears, and fastings, as the proud Pharisees and those wrangling hypocrites in

Isaiah 58:1–3.

It was a very proud saying of one, "I will not have heaven but at a price." Therefore, vain glory is well called a pleasant thief and the sweet spoiler of spiritual excellencies.

12. A Humble Soul Glorifies God in Afflictions

Daniel, the three children, the apostles, and those worthies of whom this world was not worthy. They were not anxious about getting out of affliction but studious about how to glorify God in their afflictions. They were willing to be anything and to bear anything so that in everything, God might be glorified. They made it their business to glorify God in the fire, in prison, in the den, on the rack, and under the sword. "Lord," the humble soul says, "do but keep down my sins, and keep up my heart in the way of honoring of you under all my troubles, and then my troubles will be no troubles, my afflictions will be no afflictions. Though my burdens are doubled, and my troubles be multiplied, yet do but help me to honor you by believing in you, by waiting on you, and by submitting to you, and I shall sing care away, and shall say it is enough."

When a proud man is under troubles and afflictions, his head and heart are full of plots and projects on how to get off his chains and to get out of the furnace. A proud heart will say anything, and do anything, and be anything to free himself from the burdens which press him, as you see in Pharaoh. But a humble soul is willing to bear the cross as long as he can get strength from heaven to kiss the cross, to bless God for the cross, and to glorify God under the cross (John 1:20–21).

13. A Humble Soul Is Satisfied

A little will satisfy nature; less will satisfy grace, but nothing will satisfy a proud man's lusts. "Lord," the humble soul says, "if you will but give me bread to eat and clothing to put on, you shall be my God (Gen. 28:20–22)." "Let the men of the world," the humble soul says, "take the world in all its greatness and glory and divide it among themselves.

Let me have much of Christ and heaven in my heart and food convenient to support my life—and it shall be enough." "For when they are humbled you say, 'It is because of pride;' but he saves the lowly" (Job 22:29). Or as the Hebrew has it, "him who has low eyes," noting to us that a humble soul looks not after high things. So, in Psalm 131:1–2, "Lord, my heart is not lifted up; my eyes are not raised too high." But how do you know that, David? "Why," he says, "I do not occupy myself with things too great and too marvelous for me. But I calmed and quieted my soul like a weaned child with its mother; like a weaned child is my soul within me." As a great shoe fits not a little foot, nor a great sail a little ship, nor a great ring a little finger, so a great estate fits not a humble soul.

A proud soul is a content with nothing. A crown could

not content Ahab, but he must have Naboth's vineyard, though he swims to it in blood. A humble soul is more contented and satisfied with Daniel's vegetables and John's clothes made of camel's hair than proud princes are with their glistening crowns and golden scepters.

14. A Humble Soul Rejoices in the Acts of Others

A humble Moses could say when Eldad and Medad prophesied in the camp, "Would that all the Lord's people were prophets, that the Lord would put his Spirit on them" (Num. 11:26–30). So humble Paul said, "Whether short or long, I would to God that not only you but also all who hear me this day might become such as I am—except for these chains" (Acts 26:29). I heartily wish and pray for your own sake, that not only in a low but in an eminent degree, both you and all that are here present, were as far Christians as I am, only I would not wish them imprisoned as I am.

A humble soul has no envy in spiritual things. One may have as much of spirituals as another, and all alike. So in 1 Thessalonians 1:2–3, "We give thanks to God always for all of you, constantly mentioning you in our prayers, remembering before our God and Father your work of faith and labor of love and steadfastness of hope in our Lord Jesus Christ." In 2 Thessalonians 1:2–4,

> Grace to you and peace from God our Father and the

Lord Jesus Christ. We ought always to give thanks to God for you, brothers, as is right, because your faith is growing abundantly, and the love of every one of you for one another is increasing. Therefore, we ourselves boast about you in the churches of God for your steadfastness and faith in all your persecutions and in the afflictions that you are enduring.

Ezekiel can commend Daniel, his contemporary, matching him with Noah and Job for his power in prayer. And Peter highly praises Paul's epistles, though he had been sharply reproved in one of them (Ezek. 14:14; 2 Peter 3). Oh, but proud souls will be still casting disgrace and contempt upon those excellencies in others, which they lack in themselves.

A proud cardinal, in Luther's time, said, "Indeed, a reformation is needful, and to be desired—but that Luther, a rascally friar, should be the man should do it, is intolerable." Pride is like certain flies who especially consume the fairest wheat and the most beautiful roses.

This age is full of such monsters who envy every light which outshines their own and who throw dirt upon the graces and excellencies of others that only themselves may shine. Pride is renowned both at subtraction and at multiplication.

A proud heart always prizes himself above the market. He reckons his own pence for pounds and others' pounds for pence. He looks upon his own counters as gold and upon others' gold as counters. All pearls are counterfeit but those which he wears.

15. A Humble Soul Bears Wrongs

The humble soul knows that vengeance is the Lord's and that he will repay (Ps. 94:1). The humble soul loves not to take the sword in his own hand (Rom. 12:19). He knows the day is coming, wherein the Lord will give his enemies two blows for one, and here he rests. A humble soul, when wrongs are offered, is like a man with a sword in one hand and a salve in the other—he could wound but will heal.

Malicious witnesses rise up; they ask me of things that I do not know. They repay me evil for good; my soul is bereft. But I, when they were sick—I wore sackcloth; I afflicted myself with fasting; I prayed with head bowed on my chest. I went about as though I grieved for my friend or my brother; as one who laments his mother, I bowed down in mourning. But at my stumbling they rejoiced and gathered; they gathered together against me; wretches whom I did not know tore at me without ceasing; like profane mockers at a feast, they gnash at me with their teeth (Ps. 35:11–16).

The Scripture abounds in instances of this nature. I may truly say of the humble soul what Tully said of Caesar, that he forgot nothing but injuries. Julius Caesar, in whose time Christ was born, bid Catullus, the railing poet, to supper to show that he had forgiven him.

Dionysus, having treated Plato poorly at the court, when he was gone, fearing lest he should write against him, he sent after him to bid him not to write against him. Replied Plato, "Tell Dionysus that I have not so much time as to think of him." So humble, wronged souls have no time to think of the wrongs and injuries that others do them.

John Foxe, who wrote the *Book of Martyrs*, would be sure to do him a kindness who had done him an injury, so that it used to be a proverb, "If a man would have Mr. Foxe do him a kindness, let him do him an injury." A humble soul is often in looking over the wrongs and injuries that he has done to God, and the sweet and tender treatment of God towards him notwithstanding those wrongs and injuries; and this wins him and works him to be more willing and ready to bear wrongs, and forgive wrongs, than to revenge any offered wrongs.

16. A Humble Soul Is Teachable

A child shall lead the humble soul in the way that is good; he cares not how low and contemptible the person is a guide or an instructor to him.

Apollos, an eloquent man, and mighty in the Scripture, a master in Israel, and yet sits by an Aquila, a tent-maker, and Priscilla, his wife, to be instructed by them (Acts 18:24–26). Sometimes the poorest and the lowest

Christian may, for counsel and comfort, be good to another, as Moses was to Aaron. As a humble soul knows that the stars have their situation in heaven, though sometimes he sees them by their reflection in a puddle, in the bottom of a well, or in a stinking ditch. So, he knows that godly souls, though ever so poor, low, and contemptible, as to the things of this world, are fixed in heaven, in the region above. And therefore, their poverty and baseness is no bar to hinder him from learning of them (Eph. 2:6).

Though John was poor in the world, yet many humble souls did not disdain but rejoice in his ministry. Christ lived poor and died poor (Matt. 8:20). As he was born in another man's house, so he was buried in another man's tomb. Those who were meek and lowly in heart counted it their heaven, their happiness, to be taught and instructed by him.

17. A Humble Soul Lives in Thankfulness

Gratitude is the greatest, yes, the mother of all virtues. "The Lord gave, and the Lord has taken away; blessed be the name of the Lord" (Job 1:21). He does not cry out upon the Sabeans and the Chaldeans, but he looks through all secondary causes and sees the hand of God; and then he lays his hand upon his own heart, and sweetly sings it out, "The Lord gives, and the Lord takes, blessed be the name of the Lord."

A humble soul, in every condition, blesses God. As the

apostle commands, in 1 Thessalonians 5:18, "Give thanks in all circumstances." "When reviled, we bless; when persecuted, we endure" (1 Cor. 4:12). The language of a humble soul is: "If it is your will that I should be in darkness, I will bless you. If it is your will that I should be again in the light, I will bless you. If you comfort me, I will bless you. If you afflict me, I will bless you. If you make me poor, I will bless you. If you make me rich, I will bless you. If you give me the least mercy, I will bless you. If you give me no mercy, I will bless you." A humble soul is quick-sighted. He sees the rod in a Father's hand. He sees honey upon the top of every correcting rod, and so can bless God. He sees sugar at the bottom of the bitterest cup, which God puts into his hand. He knows that God's house of correction is a school of instruction, and so he can sit down and bless when the rod is upon his back.

A humble soul knows that the design of God in all is his instruction, his reformation, and his salvation. The Jews have a proverb, that we must leap up to Mount Gerizim, which was a mount of blessings, but creep into Mount Ebal, which was a mount of curses, to show that we must be ready to bless—but backward to curse. A humble soul can extract one contrary out of another, honey out of the rock, gold out of iron. Afflictions to humble souls are the Lord's plow, the Lord's harrow, the Lord's flail, the Lord's drawing-plaster, the Lord's pruning knife, the Lord's portion, the Lord's soap. Therefore, they can sit down and bless the Lord and kiss the rod.

It was a sweet saying of John Bradford, "If the queen gives me my life, I will thank her; if she banishes me, I will thank her; if she burns me, I will thank her; if she condemns me to perpetual imprisonment, I will thank her." Ay, this is the temper of a humble heart. A humble soul knows that to bless God in prosperity is the way to increase it and to bless God in adversity is the way to remove it.

A humble soul knows that if he blesses God under mercies—he has paid his debt. But if he blesses God under crosses—he has made God a debtor. But oh, the pride of men's hearts, when the rod is upon their backs! You have many professors who are seemingly humble while the sun shines, while God gives, and smiles, and strokes; but when his smiles are turned into frowns, when he strikes and disciplines. Oh, the murmurings! Oh, the disputings! The frettings! And wranglings of proud souls! They always kick when God strikes.

18. A Humble Soul Bears Reproof

"Like a gold ring or an ornament of gold is a wise reprover to a listening ear" (Prov. 25:12). A seasonable reproof falling upon a humble soul has a redoubled grace with it. It is an earring of gold, and as an ornament of fine gold, or as a diamond in a diadem.

A humble David can say, "Let a righteous man strike

me—it is a kindness; let him rebuke me—it is oil for my head" (Ps. 141:5). David compares the faithful reproof of the righteous to the excellent oil which they used on their heads. Some translate it, "Let it never cease from my head." That is, let me never lack it, and so the original will bear too, I would never lack reproofs, whatever I lack: "Yet my prayer is continually against their evil deeds." "I will require their reproofs with my best prayers in the day of their calamity," David says. Whereas a proud heart will neither pray for such as reprove them, but in their calamities will most insult over them. Oil is here metaphorically taken for words of reproof, which may be said figuratively to break the head.

Some translate it more emphatically: "The more they do, the more I shall think myself bound unto them." "Do not reprove a scoffer, or he will hate you; reprove a wise man, and he will love you. Give instruction to a wise man, and he will be still wiser" (Prov. 9:8–9). "Reprove a man of understanding, and he will gain knowledge" (Prov. 19:25). You know how sweetly David carries it towards Abigail (1 Sam. 25:32–33). She wisely meets him and puts him in mind of what he was going about, and he falls a-blessing of her presently: "Blessed be the Lord, the God of Israel, who sent you this day to meet me! Blessed be your discretion, and blessed be you, who have kept me this day from bloodguilt" (1 Sam. 25:32–33). I was resolved in my passion, and in the heat of my spirit, that I would not leave

HUMILITY

a man alive, but blessed be God and blessed be your counsel!

A humble soul can sit down and bless God under reproofs. A humble soul is able to bear reproofs with much wisdom and patience. Oh, but a proud heart cannot bear reproofs. He scorns the reprover and his reproofs too. Manasseh, king of Judah, at the age of eighteen, being reproved by the aged princely prophet Isaiah, caused him to be sawn in half with a wooden saw; for which cruel act, among his other sins, he was sorely punished by God (2 Chron. 33:11).

"A scoffer does not like to be reproved; he will not go to the wise" (Prov. 15:12). "They hate him who reproves in the gate, and they abhor him who speaks the truth" (Amos 5:10). As Ahab hated good Micaiah, and Herod did John Baptist, and the Pharisees hated our Savior (Luke 16:13). Christ, in his dealings with the covetous Scribes and Pharisees, lays the law home and tells them plainly that they could not serve God and mammon. Here Christ strikes at their right eye, but how do they hear this? "The Pharisees, who were lovers of money, heard all these things, and they ridiculed him" (Luke 16:14). The Pharisees did not simply laugh at Christ but also gave external signs of scorn in their countenance and gestures. They blew their nose at him, for that is the meaning of the original word. By their gestures, they demonstrated their horrid deriding of him. They fleered and jeered when they should have feared and trembled at the wrath to come: "For it is precept upon precept, precept upon precept, line upon line, line upon line, here a little, there a little" (Isa 28:10). One observes that that was a scoff put upon the prophet and is as if they should say, "Here is nothing but precept upon precept, line upon line." And, indeed, the very sound of the words in the original carries a taunt, as scornful people, by the tone of their voice and rhyming words, scorn at such as they despise. Pride and passion, and other vices, in these days, go armed; touch them ever so gently, yet, like the nettle, they will sting you, and if you deal with them openly, roughly, cuttingly, as the apostle speaks, they will swagger with you, as the Hebrew did with Moses: "Who made you a judge over us?" (Ex. 2:14). And thus, much for the properties of a humble soul.

"Humble yourselves before the Lord, and he will exalt you."

JAMES 4:10

TWO

*The Reasons Why the
Best Are the Most Humble*

Great Debtors to God

There is no man on earth who sees himself such a debtor to God—as the humble man. Every smile makes him a debtor to God, and every good word from heaven makes him a debtor to God. He looks upon all his temporal mercies—health, wealth, wife, child, and friend, and sees himself deeply indebted for all. He looks upon his spiritual mercies and sees himself a great debtor to God for them; he looks upon his graces and sees himself a debtor for them. He looks upon his experiences and sees himself a debtor for them. He looks upon all his privileges and sees himself a debtor for them. He looks upon all his blessings and sees himself a debtor for them.

HUMILITY

A humble soul sees himself so much in debt for mercies in hand, and mercies in hope—that he cannot sleep without blessing and admiring of God. The more mercy he has received, the more he looks upon himself indebted and obliged to pay duty and tribute to God. He says, "What shall I render to the Lord for all his benefits towards me? I see myself wonderfully indebted." Well, what then? Why, "I will take the cup of salvation, and call upon the name of the Lord. I will pay my vows unto the Lord, in the presence of all his people." David proclaimed,

> Bless the Lord, O my soul, and all that is within me, bless his holy name! Bless the Lord, O my soul, and forget not all his benefits, who forgives all your iniquity, who heals all your diseases, who redeems your life from the pit, who crowns you with steadfast love and mercy, who satisfies you with good so that your youth is renewed like the eagle's (Ps. 103:1–5).

A humble soul knows that it is proud of being more in debt than another. "It is true," he says, "I have this and that mercy in possession, and such and such mercies in reversion; but by all, I am the more a debtor to God." Humble souls cast the pearl of praise into the bosom of God for all his favors towards them.

A humble soul wonder to see men that are so much indebted to God for mercies, as many are, and yet sleep so quietly, and be so mindless and careless in blessing and praising of God. There is nothing, says one, which endures so small a time as the memory of mercies received; and the greater they are, the more commonly they are recompensed with ingratitude.

A Taste for God

In 1 Peter 2:2–3, "Like newborn infants, long for the pure spiritual milk, that by it you may grow up into salvation—if indeed you have tasted that the Lord is good." The best men on this side heaven have but a taste. He is but in a tasting, desiring, hungering, thirsting, and growing condition. "These are but the outskirts of his ways, and how small a whisper do we hear of him" (Job 26:14). So in 1 Corinthians 13:9–10, 12, "For we know in part and we prophesy in part…now we see in a mirror dimly, but then face to face." The Lord gives out but little of himself here, we have but a taste of divine sweetness here, we see but the back-parts of God. But the day is not far off when we shall see his face. The best of Christ is reserved until last—as the sweetest honey lies in the bottom. Our greatest knowledge here is to know that we know nothing.

The Rabbis in their comments upon Scripture, when they meet with hard knots that they cannot explain, they solve all with this, "When Elijah comes, he will resolve all things." The best men are in the dark and will be in the dark—until the Lord comes to shine forth upon them in more grace and glory. The best men on this side heaven are narrow vessels, and they are able to receive and take in but little of God. The best men are so full of the world, and the vanities thereof, that they are able to take in but little of God. Here God gives his people some tastes, that they may not faint; and he gives them but a taste, that they may long to be at their eternal home, that they may keep humble, that they may sit loose from things below, that they may not break and despise bruised reeds, and that heaven may be the sweeter to them at last.

Dwelling Upon the Worst Part

A third reason why the best men are the most humble, and that is, because the best men dwell more upon their worser part, their ignoble part.

In Isaiah 6:5, "I am a man of unclean lips," says that humble soul. So humble Job cries out of the iniquity of his youth (Job 13:26; 40:5). Humble David sighs out, "My sin is ever before me" (Ps. 51:3). So humble Paul, complains that he "has a law in his members warring against the law of his mind, and leading him captive to the law of sin;" and that, "when he would do good, evil was present with him" (Rom. 7:22–23). A humble soul sees that he can stay no more from sin than the lungs can from breathing, and the pulse from beating. He sees his heart and life to be fuller of sin than the sky is of stars, and this keeps him humble. He sees that sin is so bred in the bone, that until his bones, as Joseph's, be carried out of the Egypt of this world, it will remain. Every day he finds that these Jebusites and Canaanites are as thorns in his eyes and as goads in his sides. He finds sin an ill inhabitant, which he cannot get rid of, until the house is destroyed. As the fretting leprosy in the walls of the house would remain until the house itself was demolished. As Hagar would dwell with Sarah until she beat her out of doors, so will sin dwell with grace until death beats it out of doors. Though sin and grace were never born together and though they shall not die together, yet while the believer lives, these two must live together and this keeps them humble.

As the peacock, looking upon his black feet, lets fall his plumes—so the poor soul, when he looks upon his black feet, the vanity of his mind, the body of sin that is in him—his proud spirit falls low.

Epaminondas, an Athenian captain, being asked why he was so sad the day after a great victory, answered, "Yesterday I was tickled with much vein glory; therefore I correct myself for it today." That is the temper of a humble soul. It is very observable, that the saints are pressed to take notice of their better part: "Behold, you are beautiful, my love; behold you are beautiful" (Song of Sol. 1:15). And so, "Behold you are beautiful, behold you are beautiful" (Song of Sol. 4:1). God has much ado to get a gracious heart to mind his spiritual beauty, to take notice of the inward excellency that he has wrought in it. Though "the king's daughter is all glorious within," yet God has much ado to bring her to see and take notice of her inward beauty and glory. The humble soul is more set to eye and dwell upon its deformity—than it is upon that beauty and glory that God has stamped upon it. And this makes the man little and low in his own eyes.

Beholding God

Fourthly, the best men are the most humble, because they have the clearest sight and vision of God, and have the nearest and highest communion with God.

None on earth are so near to God, and so high in their communion with God as humble souls. And as they have the clearest visions of God, so God gives them the fullest sight and knowledge of their own sinfulness and nothingness. In Job 42:5-6, "I had heard of you by the hearing of the ear, but now my eye sees you; therefore I despise myself, and repent in dust and ashes." In a vision the Lord unveils his glory to the prophet, "Woe is me!" he says, "for I am undone," or "I am cut off," why? "Because I am a man of unclean lips, and have seen the King, the Lord Almighty" (Isa. 6:1, 5). Oh, the vision that I have had of the glory of God has given me such a clear and full sight of my own vileness and baseness, that I cannot but loathe and abhor myself. When Abraham draws near to God, then he accounts himself but dust and ashes (Gen. 18:26–27). The angels that are near God, that stand before him, in humility they cover their faces with two wings, as with a double scarf (Isa. 6:2).

Holy Fear

The fifth, and last reason why those are most humble that are most holy is, because they maintain in themselves a holy fear of sinning.

As the sunshine puts out fire, so does the fear of God put out the fire of lusts. And the more this holy fear of falling is maintained, the more the soul is humbled. "A wise man fears—turns away from evil" (Prov. 14:16). "Blessed is the one who fears the Lord always, but whoever hardens his heart will fall into calamity" (Prov. 28:14). And this keeps the holy soul humble.

The reason why humble souls do keep up in themselves a holy fear of falling, is because this is the best to keep them from falling. Job fears, and conquers on the ashheap. Adam presumes, and falls in paradise. Nehemiah fears, and stands (Neh. 5:15). Peter presumes, and falls (Matt. 26:29).

"Humble yourselves, therefore,

under the mighty hand of God so

that at the proper time he

may exalt you."

1 PETER 5:6

THREE

The Motives of Humility

Is it true that the most holy souls are the most humble souls? Then this shows you, that the number of holy souls is very few. Oh, how few be there that are low in their own eyes! The number of souls that are high in the esteem of God, and low in their own esteem are very few.

Pride in these days is too prevalent. Yet pride cannot climb so high, but justice will sit above her. Bernard says that pride is the rich man's cousin. I may add, and the poor man's cousin, and the profane man's cousin, and the civil man's cousin, and the formal man's cousin, and the hypocrite's cousin; yes, all men's cousin. Pride will, therefore, sooner or later cast down and cast out.

As you would approve yourselves to be high in the account of God, as you would approve yourselves to be not only good but eminently good, keep humble. I shall endeavor to show two things: First, to lay down some motives which may work you to be humble. Secondly, to propound some directions which may further you in this work of humility.

1. Humility Is Singled Out By God

No vessels that God delights to fill like broken vessels and contrite spirits. "God opposes the proud but gives grace to the humble" (James 4:6). The Greek word for resists signifies, to set himself in battle array. God is in battle array against a proud soul, but he gives grace to the humble. The silver dews flow down from the mountains to the lowest valleys. Abraham was but dust and ashes in his own eyes, but says God, "Shall I hide from Abraham what I am about to do" (Gen. 18:17)? No, I will not. A humble soul shall be both of God's court and his counsel too. Humble Jacob, who was in his own eyes less than the least of all mercies (Gen. 32:10). What a glorious vision he had of God, when the ground was his bed, and the stone his pillow, and the hedges his curtains, and the heavens his canopy; then he saw angels ascend and descend (Gen. 28).

A humble soul who lies low, oh what sights of God has he! What glory does he behold, when the proud soul sees nothing! God pours in grace to the humble, as men pour in water into an empty vessel. He does not drop in grace into a humble heart, but he pours it in. He who is in the low pits and caves of the earth sees the stars in the sky, when they who are upon the tops of the mountains discern them not.

The altar under the law was hollow, to receive the fire, the wood, and the sacrifice. In the same way, the hearts of men, under the gospel, must be humble, empty of all spiritual pride and self-conceitedness, that so they may receive the fire of the Spirit, and Jesus Christ, who offered himself for a sacrifice for our sins.

Humility is both a grace and a vessel to receive grace. There are none who see so much need of grace as humble souls. There are none who prize grace like humble souls. There are none who improve grace like humble souls. Therefore, God singles out the humble soul to fill him to the brim with grace when the proud is sent empty away.

2. Humility Best Befits Christians

Faith is the champion of grace and love the nurse grace, but humility the beauty of grace. "Be clothed with humility" (1 Pet. 5:5). The Greek word imports that humility is the ribbon or string which ties together all those precious pearls—the rest of the graces. If this string breaks, they are all scattered.

The Greek word that is rendered clothed, comes from another Greek word that signifies to knit, and tie knots, as nimble women used to do of ribbons to adorn their heads and bodies as if humility were the knot of every virtue, the grace of every grace. Chrysostom calls humility the root, mother, nurse, foundation, and "bond of all virtue." Basil calls it "the storehouse and treasury of all good." For what is the scandal and reproach of religion at this day? Nothing more than the pride of professors. Is not this the language of most? They are great professors, oh but very proud! They are great hearers, they will run from sermon to sermon, and cry up this man, and cry up that man, oh but proud! They are great talkers, but as proud as the devil! Oh, that you would take the counsel of the apostle, "Be clothed with humility." "Put on then, as God's chosen ones, holy and beloved, compassionate hearts, kindness, humility, meekness, and patience" (Col. 3:12). It is reported of the crystal, that it has such a virtue in it, that the very touching of it quickens other stones, and puts a luster and beauty upon them. So does humility put a luster upon every grace.

3. Humility Draws the Heart of God and Man

In Isaiah 57:15, "For thus says the One who is high and lifted up, who inhabits eternity, whose name is Holy: 'I dwell in the high and holy place, and also with him who is of a contrite and lowly spirit, to revive the spirit of the lowly, and to revive the heart of the contrite.'" The Lord singles out the humble soul of all others to make him a habitation for himself. Here is a wonder! God is on high, and yet the higher a man lifts up himself, the farther he is from God, and the lower a man humbles himself, the nearer he is to God. Of all souls, God delights most to dwell with the humble, for they do most prize and best improve his precious presence.

In Proverbs 29:23, "One's pride will bring him low, but he who is lowly in spirit will obtain honor." "The reward for humility and fear of the Lord is riches and honor and life" (Prov. 22:4). The Hebrew is, "The heel of humility." Riches and honor follow humility at the very heels. One of the ancients used to say that humility is the first, second, and third grace of a Christian.

Humility is a very drawing grace. It draws men to think well and speak well of Christ, the gospel, and the people of God. It makes the very world to say, "Ay, these are Christians indeed. They are full of light, and yet full of lowliness. They are high in worth, and yet humble in heart. Oh, these are the crown and the glory of religion."

A humble soul is like the violet, which by its fragrant smell, draws the eye and the hearts of others to him. "They are the greatest in the kingdom of heaven" (Matt. 18:4). He who is least in his own account is always greatest in God's, and in godly men's account.

4. Humility Keeps Down Pride

Man cannot possibly be kept up, whose spirit is not kept down, as you may clearly see in Pharaoh, Haman, Herod, and Nebuchadnezzar. All the world could not keep them up, because their spirit was not kept down.

"A man's pride shall bring him low" (Prov. 29:27), for it sets God against him, and angels against him, and men against him. Yes, even those who are as proud as himself. It is very observable that whereas one drunkard loves another, one swearer loves another, and one thief loves another, and one unclean person loves another. Yet, one proud person cannot endure another—but seeks to undermine him, that he alone may carry the commendations, the praise, the promotion. It is storied of the Romans, that were the proudest people on the earth, that they reckoned it as a parcel of their praise, that they brought down the proud. All the world will not keep up those people who do not keep down their spirits.

Oh, that professors would think of this in these days in which we live. All the world shall not keep up those who do not keep down their own spirits. The very design of God is to stain the pride of all human glory, and to bring into contempt the proud of the earth. Therefore, now if men in our days shall grow proud and high, under divine mercies, justice will be above them, and turn their glory into shame, and lay their honor in the dust. If your pride rises with your outward good you will certainly fall, and great will be your fall.

5. Humility Fixes the Eye Upon Jesus
Christ by his example labors to provoke his disciples to

keep humble, and to walk lowly (John 13:4–5). He rises and washes his disciples' feet and mark what he aims at in that behavior of his,

> You call me Teacher and Lord, and you are right, for so I am. If I then, your Lord and Teacher, have washed your feet, you also ought to wash one another's feet. For I have given you an example, that you also should do just as I have done to you (John 13:12–15).

"Imitate my example" Christ says. Example is the most powerful rhetoric. The highest and noblest example should be very quickening and provoking. Here you have the greatest, the noblest example of humility, that was ever read or heard of. Upon consideration of this great and eminent example of Christ's humility, a godly man cried out, "You have overcome me, O Lord! You have overcome my pride. This example of yours has mastered me! Oh, that we could say with this good man, you have overcome, O Lord, you have overcome our proud hearts, by this example you have overmastered our lofty spirits!"

This example of Christ's humility you have further set forth, "Who, though being in the form of God," that is, in the nature and essence of God, being truly God, clothed with divine glory and majesty as God, "did not count equality," it being his right by nature, "to be equal with

God" (Phil. 2:6-8). The Greek words that are rendered, "he did not count equality," import that he made it not a matter of triumph or ostentation to be equal with God, it being his right by nature, and therefore the challenging of it could be no usurpation of another's right of taking to himself that which was not his own. "Did not count equality." The Greek is equals, that is, every way equal not a secondary and inferior God, as the Arians would have him. "But emptied himself," verse 7. That is, he suspended and laid aside his glory and majesty, or disrobed himself of his glory and dignity, and became a sinner, both by imputation and by reputation, for our sakes.

And verse 8, "he humbled himself." This Sun of righteousness went ten degrees back in the dial of his Father that he might come to us with healing under his wings. "By becoming obedient to the point of death, even death on a cross." In these words, there is a kind of gradation. For it is more to become obedient than to humble himself, and more to yield unto death than to become obedient, and yet more to be crucified than simply to die. For it was to submit himself to a most painful, ignominious, and cursed death. "He became obedient." That is, to his dying day, his whole life being nothing but a continual death.

That you would never leave pondering upon that glorious example of Christ's humility until your hearts be made humble, like the heart of Christ. That that sweet word of Christ, might stick upon all your hearts, "Take my yoke upon you, and learn from me, for I am gentle and lowly in heart, and you will find rest for your souls" (Matt. 11:29).

Bonaventure engraved this sweet saying of our Lord, "Learn of me for I am meek and lowly in heart," in his study. And oh, that this saying was engraved upon all your foreheads, upon all your hearts! Oh, that it was engraved upon the dishes you eat in, the cups you drink in, the seats you sit on, the beds you lie on. It was a good law that the Ephesians made, that men should propound to themselves the best patterns, and ever bear in mind some eminent man.

Oh, when you look upon this glorious example of Christ, say, "the Lord Jesus' example shall be that my soul shall imitate."

6. Humility Frees One of Despair

When there are ever such great storms without humility will cause a calm within. There are a great many storms abroad, and there is nothing which will put the soul into a quiet condition but humility. A humble soul says, "Who am I, that I may not be despised? Who am I, that I may not be reproached, abused, slighted, neglected?" That which will break a proud man's heart, will not so much as break a humble man's sleep. In the midst of a storm, a humble soul is still in a calm. When proud hearts are at their wit's ends, stamping, swearing, and complaining at God, and man, and providence. A humble soul is quiet

HUMILITY

and still, like a ship in a harbor. Shimei comes railing and cursing of David, and calls him a bloody man, and a man of Belial, that is, a renegade, one who being desperately wicked had shaken off the yoke of government and would be under no law (2 Sam. 16:6, 13). So, the Hebrew word for renegade signifies men without yoke, or lawless. It signifies most flagitious men, and notorious and desperately wicked, stigmatized villains, even incarnate devils; and yet David remains silent, though urged by his mighty men to revenge himself. Oh, how would this cursing and railing have maddened and broken many a proud man's heart, and yet it stirs not David.

After one eminent believer was extremely persecuted, he had an opportunity to seek revenge, but he would not. "For," he says, "We must suffer more for Christ than this." The humble soul says, "What though I am thus and thus wronged? What though I have an opportunity for revenge? Yet I must suffer more than this for Christ." A humble soul, when wrongs are done to him, is like a man with a sword in one hand and salve in another, he could kill but will cure.

One wondering at the patience and humble demeanor of Socrates, towards one who reviled him, Socrates said, "If we should meet one whose body were more unsound than ours, should we be angry with him, and not rather pity him? Why then should we not do the like to him whose soul is more diseased than ours?" A humble soul, when he meets with this and that wrong from men, he knows that their souls are diseased, and that rather moves him to pity than to revenge wrongs offered. A proud heart swells and grows big when in the least wronged and is ready to call for fire from heaven and to take any opportunity for revenge of wrongs offered. "No man so abused as I, no man thus styled as I," says the proud soul. Oh, but a humble soul in patience possesses himself in all trials and storms.

7. Humility Exalts

He who is most humble is and shall be most exalted and most honored. No way to be high, like this of being low. Moses was the meekest man on earth, and God made him the most honorable, calling of him up unto himself into the mount, making known his glory to him, and making of him the leader of his people Israel. Gideon was very little in his own eyes; he was the least of his father's house in his own apprehension, and God exalts him, making him the deliverer of his Israel.

It was a good saying of one, "will you be great? Begin from below." As the roots of the tree descend so the branches ascend. The lower any man is in this sense, the higher shall that man be raised. "Whoever exalts himself will be humbled, and whoever humbles himself will be exalted" (Matt. 23:12). God, who is wisdom itself, has said it, and he will make it good, though you see no ways how it should be made good. The lowest valleys have the blessing of fruitfulness, while the high mountains are barren. "Before destruction a man's heart is haughty, but humility comes before honor" (Prov 18:12). David came not to the kingdom until he could truly say, "Lord, my heart is not lifted up; my eyes are not raised too high" (Ps. 131:1–2). Abigail was not made David's wife until she thought it honor enough to wash the feet of the lowest of David's servants (1 Sam. 25). Moses must be forty years a stranger in Midian before he became king in Jeshurun. He must be struck sick to death in the wilderness before he goes to Pharaoh on that noble embassage.

It was a sweet observation of Luther, that for the most part when God set him upon any special service for the good of the church, he was brought low by some fit of sickness or other. Surely, as the lower the ebb the higher the tide. So the lower any descend in humility, the higher they shall ascend in honor and glory. The lower this foundation of humility is laid, the higher shall the roof of honor be overlaid. If you would turn spiritual purchasers of honor, or of whatever else is good there is no way like this of humility.

We live in times wherein men labor to purchase honor. Some by their money, others by their friends, others by making themselves slaves to the lusts of men, others by the shedding of their blood in battle, and many by giving themselves up to all manner of baseness and wickedness, whereby their carnal ends may be attained, and themselves exalted. But these men and their honor will quickly be laid in the dust. Oh, but the readiest, the surest, the safest, the sweetest way to attain to true honor is to be humble, to lie low. Humility makes a man precious in the eye of God. He who is little in his own account is great in God's esteem.

8. Humility Keeps the Soul Free from Satan's Snares

As you may see in the three children in Daniel, and in those worthies in Hebrews 11, "of whom this world was not worthy." As the lowest shrubs are freed from many violent gusts and blasts of wind, which shake and rend the tallest cedars. So the humble soul is free from a world of temptations, which proud and lofty souls are shaken and torn in pieces with. The devil has least power to fasten a temptation upon a humble soul. He who has a gracious measure of humility, is neither affected with Satan's temptations nor terrified with Satan's threatenings. The golden chain does not allure him nor does the iron chain daunt him.

A proud heart is as easily conquered as tempted as easily vanquished as assaulted. But the humble soul, when tempted, says with that worthy convert, "I am not the man that I once was." There was a time when my heart was proud and lifted up, and then you could no sooner knock but I opened; no sooner call but I answered; no sooner tempt but I did assent. Oh, but now the Lord taught me to be humble. I can resist, though I cannot dispute. I can fight, but not yield.

A humble soul is good at turning Satan over to the Lord Jesus, and this increases Satan's hell. It is reported of Satan, that he should say thus of a learned man, "You do always overcome me; when I would throw you down, you lift up yourself in assurance of faith; and when I would exalt and promote you, you keep yourself in humility; and so you are too hard for me." The only way to avoid cannon-shot, as they say, is to fall down flat; no such way to be freed from temptations as to keep low.

And so I am done with the first head. Namely, the motives that should move and provoke us to keep humble, to be meek, to be nothing in our own eyes.

FOUR

*Help and Direction
in the Way of Humility*

Dwell Upon God's Greatness

Nothing humbles and breaks the heart of a sinner like God's mercy and love. Souls who converse much with sin and wrath may be much terrified; but souls who converse much with grace and mercy will be much humbled. Luke 7, the Lord Jesus shows mercy to that notorious sinner and then she falls down at his feet and loves much and weeps much. In 1 Chronicles 17, it was in the heart of David to build God a house. God would not have him to do it, yet the messenger must tell David that God would build him a house and establish his Son upon the throne forever. Look into verses 15–17, and there you shall find that David lets fall such a humble speech, which he never did before God had sent him that message of advancement. "Then King David went in and sat before the Lord and said,

> Who am I, O Lord God, and what is my house, that you have brought me thus far? And yet this was a small thing in your eyes, O Lord God. You have spoken also of your servant's house for a great while to come, and this is instruction for mankind, O Lord God (2 Sam. 7:18-19).

And this sweetly and kindly melts him, and humbles him, before the Lord. Oh, if ever you would have your souls kept low dwell upon the free grace and love of God to you in Christ! As honey flows naturally from the bee, so does mercy flow naturally from God. Dwell upon the *firstness* of his love, dwell upon the *freeness* of his love, the *greatness* of his love, the *fullness* of his love, the *unchangeableness* of his love, the *everlastingness* of his love, and the *ardency* of his love. If this does not humble you, there is nothing on earth which will do it.

Dwell upon what God has undertaken for you. Dwell upon the choice and worthy gifts which he has bestowed on you; and dwell upon that glory and happiness which he has prepared for you—and then be proud if you can.

Keep Faith Upon Christ

There are two special sights of Christ, that tend much to

humble and abase a soul. The one is a sight of Christ in his misery (Zech. 12:10). And the other is a sight of Christ in his glory (Rev. 1:7; Isa. 6:1, 3, 5).

It is dangerous to be more *notion* than *motion*; to have faith in the *head* and none in the *heart*; to have an idle and not an active faith. It is not enough for you to have faith, but you must look to the acting of your faith, upon Christ as crucified, and upon Christ as glorified. Souls much in this will be very little and low in their own eyes. The great reason why the soul is no more humble is because faith is no more active. As one scale goes up, the other goes down; so as faith goes up, the heart goes down.

Labor to Kill Sin

There is the seed of all sins, of the vilest and worst of sins, in the best of men. When you see a drunkard, you may see the seed of that sin in your own nature. When you see an immoral man, the seeds of immorality you may see in your own nature. If you are not as wicked as others, it is not because of the goodness of your nature, but from the riches of God's grace. Remember this, there is not a worse nature in hell than that which is in you, and it would manifest itself accordingly, if the Lord did not restrain it. It would carry you to those horrid acts that are against the very light of nature. "By the grace of God I am what I am!" (1 Cor. 15:10). "For who sees anything different in you? What do you have that you did not receive? If then you

HUMILITY

received it, why do you boast as if you did not receive it?" (1 Cor. 4:7).

I have read of an Italian monster, who, capturing his enemy set his dagger to his heart, and made him to abjure and blaspheme the Lord, that so he might save his life. Which being done, he thrust him through and with a bloody triumph insulting over him said, "Oh, this is right noble and heroic revenge, which does not only deprive the body of temporal life—but brings also the immortal soul to endless flames everlastingly." See what natures you carry with you. It was a good saying of one of the fathers: "Other vices are in sins," says he, "but pride and high confidence is most apt to creep in upon duties well done."

There was one who was a long time tempted to three horrid sins: to be drunk, to lie with his mother, and to murder his father. Being a long time followed with these horrid temptations, at last he thought to get rid of them, by yielding to what he judged the least, and that was to be drunk; but when he was drunk, he did both lie with his mother and murder his father. Why, such a hellish nature is in every soul that breathes, and did God leave men to act according to their natures, men would be all incarnate devils, and this world a total hell.

Such is the corruption of our nature, that propound any divine good to it, it is entertained as fire by water, but propound any evil, and it is like fire to straw. It is like the foolish satyr who made haste to kiss the fire. It is like that unctuous matter, which the naturalists say that it sucks and snatches the fire to it with which it is consumed.

There was a holy man who rarely heard of other men's crimson sins, but he usually soaked the place with his tears, considering that the seeds of those very sins were in his own nature. In your nature you have that that would lead you with the Pharisees to oppose Christ; and with Judas, to betray Christ; and with Pilate, to condemn Christ; and with the soldiers, to crucify Christ. Oh, what a monster, what a devil would you prove, should God but leave you to act suitable to that sinful and woeful nature of yours!

Dwell Upon Your Imperfections

Oh the wanderings! Oh the deadness, the dullness, the fruitlessness of your spirit in religious duties! Man is a creature apt to hug himself in religious services, and to pride himself in holy duties; and to stroke himself after duties, and to warm himself by the sparks of his own fire, his own performances (Isa. 50:11). Whenever you come off from holy services, sit down, and look over the spots, blots, and blemishes which cleave to your choicest services. The fairest day has its clouds, the richest jewels their flaws, the finest faces their spots, the fairest copies their blots, and so have our finest and fairest duties. When we have done our best, we have cause to fall down at Jesus' feet, and with tears in our eyes sue out our pardon.

Never Forget Your Past

HUMILITY

In the day of your present greatness, forget not your former baseness. Humble Jacob, in the day of his prosperity, remembers his former poverty: "I am not worthy of the least of all the deeds of steadfast love and all the faithfulness that you have shown to your servant, for with only my staff I crossed this Jordan, and now I have become two camps" (Gen. 32:10). And so David, in his prosperity, remembered that his sheep-hook was changed into a scepter, and his seat of turf into a royal throne (Ps. 78:71; 1 Chron. 17). And when Joseph was a royal favorite, he remembered that he had been an imprisoned slave. And when Gideon was raised to be a savior to Israel, he remembered how God took him from the threshing-floor (Judg. 6:11), and how God changed his threshing instrument of wood into one of iron, to thresh the mountains, as God himself phrases it (Isa. 41:15).

Primislaus, the first king of Bohemia, kept his country shoes always by him, to remember from whence he was raised. Agathocles, by the furniture of his table, confessed that from a potter he was raised, to be a king of Sicily.

We live in times wherein many a man has been raised from the ash-heap to sit with princes; and oh that such were wise to remember their former low and contemptible beings, and to walk humbly before the Lord!

Otherwise, who can tell but that greater contempt shall be poured forth upon them, than that which they have poured upon princes.

View All as the Fruit of Grace

Look upon your adoption into God's family, and write this motto, 'This is the fruit of free grace!' Look upon your justification, and write this motto, 'This is the fruit of free grace!' Look upon all your graces, and write, 'These are the fruit of free grace!' Look upon your experiences, and write, 'These are the fruits of free grace!' Look upon your strength to withstand temptations, and write, 'This is the fruit of free grace!' Look upon divine power to conquer corruptions, and write, 'This is the fruit of free grace!' Look upon the bread you eat, the wine you drink, the clothes you wear and write, 'These are the fruits of free grace!' "For who sees anything different in you? What do you have that you did not receive? If then you received it, why do you boast as if you did not receive it?" (1 Cor. 4:7). Who makes you to differ?

This age is full of such proud monsters, but a humble soul sees free grace to be the spring and fountain of all his mercies and comforts. He writes *free grace* upon all his temporals, and upon all his spirituals. "By the grace of God I am what I am!" (1 Cor. 15:10).

Meditate Often

First, the great mischief that sin has done in the world. It cast angels out of heaven, and Adam out of paradise. It has laid the first cornerstone in hell and ushered in all the evils and miseries that are in the world. It has thrown down Abraham, the best believer in the world; and Noah, the most righteous man in the world; and Job, the most upright man in the world; and Moses, the meekest man in the world; and Paul, the greatest apostle in the world. Oh, the diseases, the crosses, the losses, the miseries, the deaths, the hells, which sin has brought upon the world!

Basil wept when he saw the rose, because it brought to his mind the first sin, from whence it had the prickles, which it had not while man continued in innocency, as he thought! Oh, when he saw the prickles his soul wept. So when we see, hear, or read of the blood, misery, wars, and ruins which sin has brought upon us, let us weep and lie humble before the Lord.

Secondly, meditate much on this, that many wicked men take more pains to damn their souls and go to hell than you do to save your soul and to get to heaven (Matt. 22:15).

Oh, what pains do wicked men take to damn their souls and go to hell! It is said of Marcellus, the Roman general, that he could not be quiet, neither conquered nor conqueror. Such restless wretches are wicked men. The drunkard rises up in the morning, and continues until midnight, until wine inflames him (Isa. 5:11). The unclean person wastes his time, and strength, and estate—and all to ruin his own soul.

Theotimus, being told by his physician, that if he did

not leave his lewd courses, he would lose his sight, answered, "then farewell, sweet light." What a great deal of pains does the worldling take! He rises up early, and goes to bed late, and leaves no stone unturned, and all to make himself but the more miserable in the close.

What reason have you to spend your days in weeping? When you look abroad, see what pains most men take to damn their souls and go to hell, and then consider what little pains you take to escape hell, to save your souls, and go to heaven.

Become More Acquainted With God

If ever you would keep humble, no knowledge humbles and abases like that which is inward and experimental. We live in days wherein there is abundance of notional light. Many professors know much of God notionally but know nothing of God experimentally. They know God in the history but know nothing of God in the mystery. They know much of God in the letter, but little or nothing of God in the Spirit. Therefore, it is that they are so proud and high in their own conceits, whereas he who experimentally knows the Lord is a worm and no man in his own eyes.

As the sun is necessary to the world, the eye to the body, the pilot to the ship, the general to the army, so is experimental knowledge to the humbling of a soul. Who more experimental in their knowledge than David, Job,

Isaiah, and Paul? And who are more humble than these worthies? It is a sad thing to be often eating of the tree of knowledge, but never to taste of the tree of life.

Seneca observed of the philosophers, that when they grew more learned, they were less humble. So a growth in mere notions will bring a great decay in humility and zeal, as it is too evident in these days. Well, remember this, a drop of experimental knowledge will more humble a man than a sea of notional knowledge.

Look to Christ for Strength

It is sad in these knowing times to think how few there are, who know the right way of bringing under control, the power of any sin. Most men scarcely look so high as a crucified Christ for power against their powerful sins. One soul sits down and complains, "Such a lust haunts me, I will pray it down." Another says, "Such a sin follows me, and I watch it down, or resolve it down." And so a crucified Christ is not in all their thoughts. Not but that you are to hear, pray, watch, and resolve against your sins; but above all, you should look to the acting of faith upon a crucified Christ (Ps. 10:4). It was the blood of the sacrifice and the oil that cleansed the leper in the law, and that by them was meant the blood of Christ and the grace of his Spirit, is agreed by all.

As he said of the sword of Goliath, "There is none like that," so I say, "There is none like this, for the bringing under the pride of men's hearts." The weaker the house of Saul grew, the stronger the house of David grew. The weakening of your pride will be the increase and strengthening of your humility, and therefore what the king of Syria said unto his fifty captains, "Fight neither with small nor great, but with the king of Israel." So, say I, "If you would keep humble, if you will lie low, draw forth your artillery, place your greatest strength against the pride of your souls." The death of pride will be the resurrection of humility.

"For the Lord of hosts has a day against all that is proud and lofty, against all that is lifted up— and it shall be brought low."

ISAIAH 2:12

FIVE

Concerning Pride

There are ten propositions that I shall lay down concerning pride.

1. Pride Is Most Dangerous to the Souls of Men

Pride is a sin that will put the soul upon the worst of sins. Pride is a gilded misery, a secret poison, a hidden plague. It is the engineer of deceit, the mother of hypocrisy, the parent of envy, the moth of holiness, the blinder of hearts, the turner of medicines into maladies, and remedies into diseases. It is the original and root of most of those notorious vices that are to be found among men. It was pride which put Herod upon seeking the blood of Christ. It was pride which put the Pharisees upon the persecuting of Christ. It was pride which made Athaliah destroy all the seed-royal of the house of Judah that she might reign (2 Chron. 22:10). It was pride that put Joab upon murdering treacherously, under guise of friendship, Abner (2 Sam. 3:27), and Amasa (2 Sam. 20:9–10). Zimri, out of ambition to reign, murdered Elah his Lord (1 Kings 16:8–10). Omri, out of pride and ambition to reign, when he "saw that the city was taken, he went into the citadel of the king's house and burned the king's house over him with fire and died" (1 Kings 16:18).

It is pride which has ushered in all the contentions that are in towns, cities, countries, families, and pulpits throughout the world. It was pride and ambition to reign, which put Absalom upon pursuing his father's life, from whom he had received life. A world of instances out of histories might be given, if it were needful, to further evidence this truth.

It is very remarkable, that the pride and ambition of Nebuchadnezzar did usher in the destruction of the Assyrian monarchy; and the ambition and pride of Cyrus that did usher in the overthrow of the Babylonian monarchy; and the ambition and pride of Alexander was the cause of the annihilation of the Persian monarchy; and it was the pride and ambition of the Roman commanders that was the cause of the utter subversion of the Grecian monarchy. There is no tongue which can express, nor heart which can conceive, the horrid sins and miseries which pride has ushered in among the children of men. All sin will fill a proud heart that is resolved to rise. Great sins are no sins with such a soul. He makes nothing of those very sins that would make the very heathen to blush.

2. Pride Hardens the Heart

As you may see in Pharaoh. Pride turned his heart into steel, yes, into a very rock. God strikes again and again. He sends plague upon plague, and yet the more he is plagued, the more he is hardened. His pride turned his soul into a rock. He is no more sensible of the frowns of God, the threatenings of God, the plagues, the strokes of God, than a rock. Pride had hardened his heart— he stirs not, he yields not. Proud souls are of his mind that said, "though you do convince me, yet will I not be convinced."

It was the pride of Saul that turned his heart into steel: "I have sinned," says he, "yet honor me before the people" (1 Sam. 15:30). God gave him many a blow, many a knock, and many a check, and yet after all, "Honor me before the people." Oh, how desperately was his heart hardened in pride!

In Daniel 5:18, Nebuchadnezzar's mind, says the text, "was hardened in pride." He saw the vengeance of the Almighty upon his predecessors, and God took him up, and lashed him until the blood came, and yet he made nothing of it because his heart was hardened in pride. Pride sets a man in opposition against God. Other sins are aversions from God, but this sin is a coming against God. In other sins a man flies from God, but in this sin a man flies upon God.

"God resists the proud" (James 4:6). A man does not resist another until he is set upon; the traveler does not resist until such time as the thief attacks him. Says the text, "God resists the proud." It intimates thus much to us, that the proud heart attacks God himself, and therefore God resists him. He places himself in battle array against the proud. God brings forth his battalia against the proud, and they bring forth their battalia against God. A proud heart resists and is resisted. This is flint to flint, fire to fire, yet in the day of God's wrath the proud shall be burnt up as stubble, both branch and root (Mal. 4:1).

3. Pride Shows Itself in Many Ways

First, sometimes it shows itself in the looks (Prov. 6:17). He tells you of seven things that the Lord hates, and one is a proud look. The Hebrew word there is, "The haughty eye." The haughty eye God hates. Men's hearts usually show themselves in their eyes "My heart is not lifted up; my eyes are not raised too high" (Ps. 131:1). There are such who show pride in their very looks, but the Lord looks aloof at them (Ps. 138:6).

Secondly, sometimes pride shows itself in words: "Is not this great Babylon, which I have built by my mighty power as a royal residence and for the glory of my majesty?" (Dan. 4:30). And in chapter 15, "Who is that God that shall deliver you out of my hands?" It was a very proud saying of one, "We have not so lived and deserved of God that the enemy should vanquish us." These were the proud ones, that spoke loftily, and that set their mouths against the heavens, as the psalmist speaks (Ps. 73:6, 8–9). And such a one was Henry the Second. Hearing that his city Mentz was taken, he used this proud blasphemous speech, "I shall never love God anymore, who allowed a city so dear to me to be taken away from me." Such a proud wretch, both in words and actions, was Sennacherib, as you may see in Isaiah 37:8–18.

Thirdly, sometimes pride shows itself in the clothing of the body. So, Herod's pride appeared: "Herod was arrayed in royal apparel" (Acts 12:21). "In cloth of silver," says Josephus, "which, being beaten upon by the sunbeams, dazzled the people's eyes, and drew from them that blasphemous acclamation, it is the voice of God, and not of man." The people being most commonly like the Bohemian curs, that used to fawn upon a good suit. So, the rich man in Luke 16:19, was clothed in purple, and in silk. He was commonly so clothed, it was his every day wear, as the Greek word implies.

But here a question may be asked: May not people clothe themselves according to their dignities, ranks, and places that God has put them in the world?

I answer they may, and ought so to do. If God has lifted them up in the world above others, they may wear better

HUMILITY

apparel than others (Gen 41:42; Ps. 45:13–14). I cite these scriptures so much the rather, because some, through weakness and peevishness, stumble and are not satisfied herein. There is nothing in the law of God or nature against it.

But you may say: May not people sin in their apparel? I answer yes, and that in four cases:

First, when it is not modest but carries with it provocation to lust and immorality: "The woman meets him, dressed as a prostitute" (Prov. 7:10). The Hebrew word signifies a clothing finely set and fitted to the body. And says the text, she was "wily of heart," or trussed up about the breasts, with her upper parts naked. One man reads the words, "She met him with her naked breasts," at this day too commonly used by such as would not be held harlots. Oh, what a horrid shame and reproach is it to religion, the ways of God, and the people of God, that professors should go so! One says, "that superfluous apparel is worse than whoredom, because whoredom only corrupts chastity, but this corrupts nature." Another says, "If women adorn themselves so as to provoke men to lust after them, though no ill follow upon it, yet those women shall suffer eternal damnation, because they offered poison to others, though none would drink of it."

Second, people sin in their apparel when they exceed their degree and rank in costly apparel, which is that which is condemned by the apostle (1 Tim. 2:9; 1 Pet. 3:3).

The apostle does not simply condemn the wearing of gold, but he condemns it in those who go above their degree and rank. The words are rather an admonition than a prohibition.

Third, it is sinful when it is so expensive as that it hinders works of mercy and charity. Oh, how many proud souls are there in these days that lay so expense much upon their backs, that they can spare nothing to fill the poor's bellies. Silk clothing hinders works of charity and mercy. Surely those who put on such costly ornaments upon their backs as close up the hand of charity will at last share with many in their misery.

Fourth, when persons habit themselves in strange and foreign fashions, which is the sin, shame, and reproach of many among us in these days. Now that is strange apparel which is not peculiar to the nations where men live. The Lord threatens to punish such (Zeph. 1:8), that are clothed with strange apparel. There are too many women and men in our days that are like the Egyptian temples, very gypsies, painted without and spotted within, varnish without and vermin within.

Mercury being to make a garment for the moon, as one says, could never fit her but either the garment would be too big or too little, by reason she was always increasing or decreasing. May not this be applied to the vain curiosity of too many professors in these days, whose curiosity about their clothes can never be satisfied?

I shall conclude this head with this counsel: Clothe yourselves with the silk of piety, with the satin of sanctity, and with the purple of modesty, and God himself will be a suitor to you. Let not the ornaments upon your backs speak out the vanity of your hearts.

Likewise also that women should adorn themselves in respectable apparel, with modesty and self-control, not with braided hair and gold or pearls or costly attire, but with what is proper for women who profess godliness—with good works (1 Tim. 2:9–10).

Sometimes pride shows itself by the gesture and demeanor of the body. "The daughters of Zion are haughty and walk with outstretched necks, glancing wantonly with their eyes, mincing along as they go, tinkling with their feet" (Isa. 3:16). Oh earth, do you not groan to bear such monsters as these?

Sometimes pride shows itself in contemptuous challenges of God. As Pharoah, "Who is the God of the Hebrews, that I should obey him?" (Ex. 5:2).

Sometimes pride shows itself by bragging promises, "I will pursue, I will overtake, I will divide the spoil, my desire shall have its fill of them. I will draw my sword; my hand shall destroy them" (Ex. 15:9).

4. Pride Makes a Person Most Like Satan

Pride is Satan's disease. Pride is so base a disease, that God had rather see his dearest children to be buffeted *by* Satan, than that in pride they should be *like* Satan. When Paul, in 2 Corinthians 12:7, under the abundance of revelations, was in danger of being puffed up, the Lord, rather than he would have him proud like to Satan, suffers him to be buffeted by Satan. Humility makes a man like to angels and pride makes an angel a devil. Pride is worse than the devil, for the devil cannot hurt you until pride has possessed you. If you would see the devil portrayed to the life, look upon a proud soul, for as face answers to face, so does a proud soul answer to Satan. Proud souls are Satan's apes, and none imitate him to the life like these. And oh, that they were sensible of it, before it be too late, before the door of darkness be shut upon them!

5. Pride Never Climbs High

One asked a philosopher what God was doing? He answered that his whole work was to exalt the humble and pull down the proud. It was pride which turned angels into devils; they would be above others in heaven, and therefore God cast them down to hell. The first man would know as God, and the Babel-builders would dwell as God, but justice set above them all. This truth you see verified in the justice of God upon Pharaoh, Haman, Herod, Belshazzar, and Nebuchadnezzar. All these would be very high, but justice takes the right hand of them all, and brings them down to the dust.

Yes, pride cannot climb so high in the hearts of saints,

but divine justice will be above it. Uzziah his heart was lifted up (2 Chron. 16:16), but justice smites him with a leprosy, and so he died, out of grief and sorrow. David glories in his own greatness (2 Sam. 24:1), and for this, seventy thousand fall by the hand of justice. Hezekiah's heart was lifted up, but wrath was upon him, and upon all Judah and Jerusalem for it (2 Chron. 32:25). Pride sets itself against the honor, being, and sovereignty of God, and therefore justice will in spite of all sit above her. Other sins strike at the word of God, the people of God, and the creatures of God, but pride strikes directly at the very being of God, and therefore justice will be above her.

Nebuchadnezzar was proud, and God smites his reason, and turns him into a beast. Oh, how many young professors are there in our days, who have been proud of their notions, and proud of their parts and gifts—justice has so smitten them, that they have lost that life, that sweetness, that spiritualness, which quickness what once they had, and are dried and shriveled up by a hand of justice. They are like the apples of Sodom, splendid on the outside but rotten and worthless within. Some there are who have been very shining, yet by reason of pride have fallen from a seeming excellency to be naught, and from naught to be very naught, and from very naught to be stark naught. "The Lord of hosts has purposed it, to defile the pompous pride of all glory, to dishonor all the honored of the earth" (Isa. 23:9). The Hebrew word that is here rendered *purposed*, signifies to consult, or take counsel. It is consulted and agreed upon in counsel that he will destroy your pride and show his contempt for all human greatness; and the counsel of the Lord shall stand (Ps. 33:11; Isa. 2:11–12).

> The haughty looks of man shall be brought low, and the lofty pride of men shall be humbled, and the Lord alone will be exalted in that day. For the Lord of hosts has a day against all that is proud and lofty, against all that is lifted up—and it shall be brought low (Isa. 2:11–12).

Divine justice will take the right hand of all proud ones on the earth. God bears, as I may say, a special hatred against pride. His heart hates it (Prov. 6:16–17). His mouth curses it (Ps. 119:21), and his hand plagues it. As you have seen in the former instances, and as you may see further in these following instances:

The king of Egypt, which Jeremiah prophesied against, in his forty-fourth chapter, was so puffed up with pride, that he boasted his kingdom was so surely settled, that it could not be taken from him either by God or man. Not long after he was taken in battle by Amasis, one of his own subjects, and hanged.

Dionysius the tyrant said in the pride of his heart, that his kingdom was bound to him with chains of adamant;

but time soon confuted him, for he was driven out, and forced to teach a school at Corinth for a poor living.

Cares, a soldier, being proud of his valor, because he had given Cyrus a great wound, shortly after he ran mad. In all ages there are notable instances to prove that pride has not got so high, but justice has set above her.

6. Pride Is the Most Dangerous of Sins

Spiritual pride is the lifting up of the mind against God. It is a tumor and swelling in the mind and lies in despising and slighting of God—his word, promises, and ordinances, and in the lifting up of a man's self, by reason of birth, breeding, wealth, honor, place, relation, gifts or graces, and in despising of others. Of this spiritual pride Habakkuk speaks, "His heart that is lifted up in him, is not upright" (Hab. 2:4). "Everyone who is arrogant in heart is an abomination to the Lord; be assured, he will not go unpunished" or, who "lifts up his heart against God" (Prov. 16:5).

Satan is subtle. He will make a man proud of his very graces. He will make him proud that he is not proud. Pride grows with the decrease of other sins and thrives by their decay. Other sins are nourished by poisonous roots, as adultery is nourished by idleness, and gluttony and murder by malice and envy, but this white devil, spiritual pride, springs from good duties and good actions towards God and man. Spiritual pride is a very great enemy to the good and salvation of man. Pride is like a very great swelling, which unfits men for any service.

Again, spiritual pride is a very great enemy to the good and salvation of men. The Greek word signifies swelling, for pride is like a great swelling in the body, which unfits it for any good service. "You refuse to come to me that you may have life" (John 5:40). And, "How can you believe, when you receive glory from one another and do not seek the glory that comes from the only God?" (John 5:44). Christ blesses his Father that he had "hidden these things from the wise and understanding and revealed them to little children" (Matt. 11:25). It is the pride of men's hearts that makes them throw off ordinances, as poor and low things, when, alas, in their practices they live below the power, beauty, glory, and holiness of the least and lowest ordinance. There is more holiness, purity, and glory manifested in the lowest administrations of Christ than is held forth by them, in their highest practices.

7. Pride Makes Man Act Low

As you may see in Pharaoh, Haman, Herod, Nebuchadnezzar. It makes men bedlams. It was pride which made Hildebrand to cause Henry the Fourth to stand three days at his gate, with his wife and his child, barefooted. It was pride that made Adonibezek cause seventy kings, with their thumbs and great toes cut off (Judg. 1:5–7), to gather their food under his table. Oh! What wretched unmanly acts has the pride of many persons put them upon.

8. Pride Creates a Poor Spirit

Interesting is the parable of Jotham: the best trees refused to be king, but the bramble wanted it; and did hope and aspire to it (Judg. 9:15). So, in 2 Kings 14:9, "A thistle on Lebanon sent to a cedar on Lebanon, saying, 'Give your daughter to my son for a wife.'" Hagar the kitchen-maid will be proud, and insult over her mistress Sarah (Gen. 21). The poor sons of Zebedee desired to sit at Christ's right hand and left (Matt. 20:20-21). And those who Job disdains to set with the dogs of his flock despise him in the day of his sorrow (Job 30:1). The foot strives to be equal with the head, the servant as the master, the cobbler as the counselor, and the peasant as the prince.

9. Pride Is a Forerunner of a Fall

"Pride goes before destruction, and a haughty spirit before a fall" (Prov. 16:18; 18:12). Herod fell from a throne of gold—to a bed of dust. Nebuchadnezzar fell from the state of a mighty king—to be a beast. Adam fell from innocency to mortality. The angels fell from heaven to hell, from felicity to misery.

10. Pride Is Always Conquered by God

You haughty ones, who think to escape, and battle it out, remember this, God will by an almighty and invincible power conquer you. When you think not of it, he will eat you like a moth.

You felt secure in your wickedness; you said, 'No one sees me;' your wisdom and your knowledge led you astray, and you said in your heart, 'I am, and there is no one besides me.' But evil shall come upon you, which you will not know how to charm away; disaster shall fall upon you, for which you will not be able to atone; and ruin shall come upon you suddenly, of which you know nothing (Isa. 47:10–11).

Impunity oftentimes causes impudency, but God's forbearance is no acquittance. The longer the hand is lifted up, the heavier will be the blow at last. Of all metals, lead is the coldest, but being melted, it becomes the hottest. Humble souls know how to apply this, and proud souls shall sooner or later experience this.

"Humble yourselves before the Lord, and he will lift you up."

JAMES 4:10

SIX

Be Clothed With Humility

Satan has his devices to destroy the saints and one great device that he has to destroy the saints is, by working them first to be strange, and then to divide, and then to be bitter and jealous, and then "to bite and devour one another" (Gal. 5:15). Our own woeful experience is too great a proof of this."

The Christian's remedy is to labor to be clothed with humility:
- Humility makes a man peaceable among brethren fruitful in well-doing, cheerful in suffering, and constant in holy walking.
- Humility fits for the highest service we owe to Christ, and yet will not neglect the lowest service to

HUMILITY

the meanest servant.
- Humility will make a man bless him that curses him, and pray for those that persecute him.
- Humility is the nurse of our graces, the preserver of our mercies, and the great promoter of holy duties.
- Humility can sweep over other men's weaknesses, and joy and rejoice over their graces.
- Humility will make a man quiet and contented in the meanest condition, and it will preserve a man from ever envying other men's prosperous condition.
- Humility honors those that are strong in grace, and puts two hands under those that are weak in grace.
- Humility makes a man richer than other men, and it makes a man judge himself the poorest among men.
- Humility will see much good abroad, when it can see but little at home.
- Humility will make a man have high thoughts of others and low thoughts of a man's self.
- Humility will make a man excellent at covering others' infirmities, and at recording their gracious services, and at delighting in their graces.
- Humility makes a man joy in every light that outshines his own, and every wind that blows others good.
- Humility is better at believing than it is at questioning

other men's happiness.

Ah, were Christians more humble, there would be less fire and more love among them than now is."

www.ingramcontent.com/pod-product-compliance
Lightning Source LLC
Chambersburg PA
CBHW072206100526
44589CB00015B/2387